DISCOVERING BIBLICAL TREASURES

UNDERSTANDING NAHUM

A Commentary on the Book of Nahum using Ancient Bible Study Methods - **UPDATED**

Michael Harvey Koplitz

TABLE OF CONTENTS

ACKNOWLEDGMENTS

This work could not have been accomplished without Dr. Anne Davis, who taught me Ancient (Hebraic) Bible study methods, and my two study partners, Rev. Dr. Robert Cook and Pastor Sandra Koplitz. We know the journey has just started and will last a lifetime. The discovery of the depths of God's Word is awaiting us to find.

Introduction

While I was attending Seminary earning my M. Div. degree, I questioned what the instructors and reference books, which were required, were saying about the Scriptures. One idea being offered then was that the Bible was full of errors and not factual. I found that attitude disturbing for seminary instructors to be teaching. After all, the Seminary experience is to train pastors to go out into God's world and preach the Bible. How can you preach the Bible if you believe what these instructors are teaching? The methods that were being taught to examine the Bible just seemed inaccurate to me.

After graduating from Seminary, I spent a lot of time reading different views about the Bible. I eventually reached the Zohar. This collection of midrash is considered the secret work of the Torah, according to Kabbalists. In addition, I read quite a bit about Messianic Judaism. Their view of the Bible is quite different from the Seminary view.

I decided that the biblical interpretation that was being taught in Seminary was not the biblical interpretation the people heard when Jesus Christ (whose Hebraic name is Yeshua) preached. I went on a quest to learn what the people of Yeshua's day heard, and what they thought when the Scriptures were read. This quest led me to Dr. Anne Davis and The Bible Learning University. Dr. Davis was in search of the same thing I was searching. She had made many discoveries that helped me in my quest. I earned the Ph.D. degree from The Bible Learning University in Hebraic Studies in Christianity concentrating on ancient Bible Studies methods.

Finally, I found someone who believed that the church has placed almost 1900 years of their theological ideas about the Scriptures, which differed from the original Hebraic thoughts, and in many places possibly misinterpreted its original meaning. What is also important to hear is that the basic tenants of Yeshua as God's Messiah, my LORD and Savior are in the Bible. My faith in Yeshua is stronger now that I have learned from Dr. Davis how to study the Scriptures in the same manner that the people did in Yeshua's day.

I have included some articles that describe the differences between Greek learning methods and Hebraic learning methods. Please do not skip by them as irrelevant, unless you are familiar with ancient Bible student method, because if you do then the analysis and commentary that follows may become difficult to understand.

Our God is vast and infinite and so is His Word. May God bless you in your discovery of what God's Word is about.

The book of Nahum was probably written around 700 BCE. Nahum gives an eyewitness account of the destruction of the great city of Nineveh. Nahum lived after Jonah. According to Jonah, Nineveh had repented of their sins. However, Nahum tells us they went back to their evil ways. The God of Israel had sent His prophets to Israel and Judah and had then sent Jonah the prophet to Nineveh. Nineveh fell in 612 BCE.

The Main Difference between the Greek Method and Hebraic Method of Teaching

Once you are aware of the two teaching styles, you will determine if you are in a class or reading a book, whether the analysis and/or teaching method is in a Greek or Hebraic method. In the Greek method, the instructor is right because of advanced knowledge. In the college situation, it is because the professor has his/her Ph.D. in some area of study, so one assumes that he or she knows everything about the topic. For example, Rodney Dangerfield played the role of a middle-aged man going to college. His English midterm was to write about Kurt Vonnegut Jr. Since he did not understand any of Vonnegut's books, he hired Vonnegut himself to the write the midterm. When it was returned to him, the English Professor told Dangerfield that whoever wrote the paper knew nothing about Vonnegut. This is an example of the Greek method of teaching. Did the Ph.D. English professor think she knew more about Vonnegut's writings than Vonnegut did?[1]

In the Greek teaching method, the professor or the instructor claims to be the authority. If you are attending a Bible study class and the class leader says, "I will teach you the only way to understand this biblical book," consider the implications. This method is common since most seminaries and Bible colleges teach a Greek method of learning, which is the same method the church has been using for centuries.

Hebraic teaching methods are different. The teacher wants the students to challenge what

---

[1] *Back to School.* Performed by Rodney Dangerfield. Hollywood: CA: Paper Clip Productions, 1986. DVD.

they hear. It is through questioning that a student can learn. In addition, the teacher wants his/her students to excel to a point where the student becomes the teacher.

It is said that if two rabbis come together to discuss a passage of Scripture, the result will be at least ten different opinions. All points of view are acceptable if the points can be supported by biblical evidence. It is permissible and encouraged for students to have multiple opinions. There is a depth to God's Word, and God wants us to find all His messages that are placed in the Scriptures.

Seeking the meaning of the Scriptures beyond the literal meaning is essential to fully understanding God's Word.[2] The Greek

---

[2] Davis, Anne Kimball. *The Synoptic Gospels*. MP3. Albuquerque:

method of learning the Scriptures has prevailed over the centuries. One problem is that only the literal interpretation of Scripture was often viewed as valid, as prompted by Martin Luther's "sola literalis" meaning that only the literal interpretation of Scripture was valid. The Fundamentalist movements of today are based on the literal interpretation of the Scripture. Therefore, they do not believe that God placed any deeper, hidden, or secret meanings in the Word.

The students of the Scriptures who learn through Hebraic training and understanding have drawn a different conclusion. The Hebrew language itself leads to different interpretations because of the construction of the language. The Hebraic method of Bible

NM: BibleInteract, 2012.

study opens avenues of thought about God's revelations in the Scripture that may have never been considered. A question may be raised about the Scripture being studied for which there may not be an immediate answer. If so, it becomes the responsibility of the learners to uncover the meaning. Also, remember that multiple opinions about the meaning of Scripture are also acceptable if they can be supported by Scripture.

Methodology

The method employed is to use First Century Scripture study methods integrated with the customs and culture of Yeshua's day to examine the Hebrew and Christian Scriptures, thus gathering a deeper understanding by learning the Scriptures in the way the people of Yeshua's day did.

In typical Rabbinic tradition, I had two study partners. Each one served a different function by looking at the research as I put it together. Rev. Dr. Robert Cook, D. Min., an ordained Elder in the United Methodist Church, has been a study partner in different areas of theology and church leadership. He became interested in Hebraic studies when I started sharing Zohar and Midrash with him. He also completed the entire Disciple program as a student and teacher. My second study partner is my wife, Sandra Koplitz, MS. Sandy and I took the instruction class on teaching the Disciple Bible study program and she takes part in the Zohar study group. Sandy is a licensed local pastor in the United Methodist Church.

The Process of Discovery

I have titled the method of analyzing a passage of Scripture in a Hebraic manner the "Process of Discovery." This method was developed by the author, bringing together the various areas of linguistic and cultural understanding. There are several sections to the process, and not all the sections apply to every passage of Scripture. The overall result of developing this process is to give the reader a framework into the ideas being presented.

The "Process of Discovery" starts with a Scripture passage. If the passage is in a poetic form, it is identified. Possible poetic techniques include parallelism, chiastic structures, and repetition. Formatting the passage in its poetic form allows the reader to visualize what the first century CE listener was hearing. Any parallelism is shown with colored text and the chiasms are labeled by their corresponding sections, for example: A, B, C, B', A'. Not all passages of the Scriptures have a poetic form.

The next step is to "question the narrative," which is accomplished by assuming the reader knows nothing about the passage. Therefore, the questions go from the simple to the complex. The next task is to identify any linguistic patterns. Linguistic patterns include, but are not limited to: irony, simile, metaphor, symbolism, idioms, hyperbole, figurative language, personification, and allegory.

Any translation inconsistencies discovered between the English NASB version and either the Hebrew or Greek versions are identified. Sometimes a Hebrew or Greek word can be translated in more than one way. Inconsistencies also can be created by the translation committee, which may have used traditional language instead of the actual translation. The decision of the translation committee can be found in the Preface or Introduction to the Bible. Perhaps some inconsistencies were intentionally added to convey some deeper meaning therefore, the inconsistencies need to be examined.

Echoes of the Hebrew Scriptures in the Christian Scripture are identified. This occurs when a passage from the Hebrew Scripture is used in the Christian Scripture or when a Mitzvah is directly discussed in the Christian Scriptures.[3] In addition, echoes can be found when Torah (Genesis through Deuteronomy) passages are used in other Hebrew Bible books. Besides echoes, cross-references are listed. A cross reference is a reference to another verse in the Scripture which can assist the reader to understand the verse that is being read.

The names of persons mentioned in the passage are listed. Many of the Hebrew names have meaning and may be associated with places or actions. Jewish parents used to name their children based on what they felt God had in store for their child. An example of this is

---

[3] Mitzvot are the 613 commandments found in the Torah that please God. There are positive and negative commandments. The list was first development by Maimonides. The full list can be found at: ttp://www.jewfaq.org/613.htm.

Abraham, whose original name was Abram, and was changed to mean eternal father (in this case Abram's name was changed by God to Abraham showing a function he was to perform). When the Hebrew Bible gives names, many of the occurrences will show something special to the reader/listener. The same importance can hold true for the names of places. The time to travel between places can supply insight to the event.

Keywords are identified in a verse when they are important to an understanding of that passage. There are no rules for selecting the keywords. Searching for other occurrences of the keywords in Scripture in a concordance is necessary to understand how the word was being used; this must be done in either Hebrew or Greek, not in English. A classic Hebraic approach is to find the usage of a word in the

Scripture by finding other verses that contain the word. The usage of a word, in its original language, is discovered by searching the Scripture in its original language. The verses that contain the word being researched are identified and a pattern for the usage of the word is discerned. Each verse is examined to see what the usage of the word is which, may reveal a pattern for the word's usage. For Hebrew words, the first usage of the word in the Scripture, especially if used in the Torah, is important. For the Greek words, the Christian Scriptures are used to determining the word usage in the Scripture. Sometimes finding the equivalent Greek word in the Septuagint then analyzing its usage in Hebrew can be very helpful.

The Rules of Hillel for Bible understanding can be used when applicable. Hillel was a Torah scholar who lived shortly before Yeshua's day. Hillel developed several rules for Torah students to interpret the Scriptures which are referred to as halachic midrash. In several cases, these rules are helpful in the analysis of the Scripture.

After the linguistic analysis is complete, an examination of the cultural implications will be examined. The culture is important because it is not specifically referenced in the biblical narratives as shown earlier.

From the linguistic analysis and the cultural understanding, it is possible to get a deeper meaning of the Scripture beyond the literal meaning of the plaintext. That is what the listeners of Yeshua's time were doing. They put the linguistics and the culture together without even having to contemplate it. They did it.

This will lead to a conclusion or a set of conclusions about what the passage is discussing. Most of the time, the Hebraic analysis leads to the desire for a deeper analysis to fully understand what Yeshua was discussing or what was happening to Him. Whatever the result, a new deeper understanding of the Scripture will be obtained.

The components of the Process of Discovery are:

Linguistics Section

> Linguistic Structure of the Scripture
>
> Discussion
>
> Questioning the Passage
>
> Main/Center Point
>
> Verse Comparison on citations or proof text
>
> Idioms

Metaphors

Symbols

Translation inconsistencies

People's names

Name of places

Word Study

Scripture cross references

Echoes

Rules of Hillel

Culture Section

Discussion

Questioning the passage culturally

Culture and Linguistics Section

Discussion

Only the sections pertinent to each chapter of Nahum are included.

Nahum Chapter 1

Language

New American Standard 1995	Hebrew
[1] The oracle of Nineveh. The book of the vision of Nahum the Elkoshite. [2] A jealous and avenging God is the LORD; The LORD is avenging and wrathful. The LORD takes vengeance on His adversaries, And He reserves wrath for His enemies. [3] The LORD is slow to anger and great in power, And the LORD will by no means leave *the guilty* unpunished. In whirlwind and storm is His way, And	מַשָּׂא נִינְוֵה סֵפֶר חֲזוֹן נַחוּם הָאֶלְקֹשִׁי: [2] אֵל קַנּוֹא וְנֹקֵם יְהוָה נֹקֵם יְהוָה וּבַעַל חֵמָה נֹקֵם יְהוָה לְצָרָיו וְנוֹטֵר הוּא לְאֹיְבָיו: [3] יְהוָה אֶרֶךְ אַפַּיִם (וּגְדוֹל־)[וּגְדָל־]כֹּחַ וְנַקֵּה לֹא יְנַקֶּה יְהוָה בְּסוּפָה וּבִשְׂעָרָה דַּרְכּוֹ וְעָנָן אֲבַק רַגְלָיו: [4] גּוֹעֵר בַּיָּם וַיַּבְּשֵׁהוּ וְכָל־הַנְּהָרוֹת הֶחֱרִיב אֻמְלַל בָּשָׁן וְכַרְמֶל וּפֶרַח לְבָנוֹן אֻמְלָל: [5] הָרִים רָעֲשׁוּ מִמֶּנּוּ וְהַגְּבָעוֹת הִתְמֹגָגוּ וַתִּשָּׂא הָאָרֶץ מִפָּנָיו וְתֵבֵל וְכָל־יֹשְׁבֵי בָהּ: [6] לִפְנֵי זַעְמוֹ מִי יַעֲמוֹד וּמִי יָקוּם בַּחֲרוֹן אַפּוֹ חֲמָתוֹ נִתְּכָה כָאֵשׁ וְהַצֻּרִים נִתְּצוּ מִמֶּנּוּ:

clouds are the dust beneath His feet.

⁴ He rebukes the sea and makes it dry; He dries up all the rivers. Bashan and Carmel wither; The blossoms of Lebanon wither.

⁵ Mountains quake because of Him And the hills dissolve; Indeed the earth is upheaved by His presence, The world and all the inhabitants in it.

⁶ Who can stand before His indignation? Who can endure the burning of His anger? His wrath is poured out like fire And the rocks are broken up by Him.

⁷ The LORD is good, A stronghold in the day of trouble, And He knows those

טֹ֣וב יְהֹוָ֔ה לְמָעֹ֖וז בְּיֹ֣ום צָרָ֑ה וְיֹדֵ֖עַ חֹ֥סֵי בֹֽו׃

⁸ וּבְשֶׁ֣טֶף עֹבֵ֔ר כָּלָ֖ה יַעֲשֶׂ֣ה מְקֹומָ֑הּ וְאֹיְבָ֖יו יְרַדֶּף־חֹֽשֶׁךְ׃

⁹ מַה־תְּחַשְּׁבוּן֙ אֶל־יְהֹוָ֔ה כָּלָ֖ה ה֣וּא עֹשֶׂ֑ה לֹֽא־תָק֥וּם פַּעֲמַ֖יִם צָרָֽה׃

¹⁰ כִּ֣י עַד־סִירִ֤ים סְבֻכִים֙ וּכְסׇבְאָ֣ם סְבוּאִ֔ים אֻכְּל֕וּ כְּקַ֥שׁ יָבֵ֖שׁ מָלֵֽא׃

¹¹ מִמֵּ֣ךְ יָצָ֔א חֹשֵׁ֥ב עַל־יְהֹוָ֖ה רָעָ֑ה יֹעֵ֖ץ בְּלִיָּֽעַל׃ ס

¹² כֹּ֣ה ׀ אָמַ֣ר יְהֹוָ֗ה אִם־שְׁלֵמִים֙ וְכֵ֣ן רַבִּ֔ים וְכֵ֥ן נָגֹ֖זּוּ וְעָבָ֑ר וְעִנִּתִ֕ךְ לֹ֥א אֲעַנֵּ֖ךְ עֹֽוד׃

¹³ וְעַתָּ֕ה אֶשְׁבֹּ֥ר מֹטֵ֖הוּ מֵעָלָ֑יִךְ וּמֹוסְרֹתַ֖יִךְ אֲנַתֵּֽק׃

¹⁴ וְצִוָּ֤ה עָלֶ֙יךָ֙ יְהֹוָ֔ה לֹא־יִזָּרַ֥ע מִשִּׁמְךָ֖ עֹ֑וד מִבֵּ֨ית אֱלֹהֶ֜יךָ אַכְרִ֗ית פֶּ֤סֶל וּמַסֵּכָה֙ אָשִׂ֣ים קִבְרֶ֔ךָ כִּ֥י קַלֹּֽותָ׃ פ

who take refuge in Him.

8 But with an overflowing flood He will make a complete end of its site, And will pursue His enemies into darkness.

9 Whatever you devise against the LORD, He will make a complete end of it. Distress will not rise up twice.

10 Like tangled thorns, And like those who are drunken with their drink, They are consumed As stubble completely withered.

11 From you has gone forth One who plotted evil against the LORD, A wicked counselor.

12 Thus says the LORD, "Though

they are at full *strength* and likewise many, Even so, they will be cut off and pass away. Though I have afflicted you, I will afflict you no longer. [13] "So now, I will break his yoke bar from upon you, And I will tear off your shackles." [14] The LORD has issued a command concerning you: "Your name will no longer be perpetuated. I will cut off idol and image From the house of your gods. I will prepare your grave, For you are contemptible." [15] Behold, on the mountains the feet of him who brings good news, Who announces peace!	

| Celebrate your feasts, O Judah; Pay your vows. For never again will the wicked one pass through you; He is cut off completely. | |

Process of Discovery

Linguistics Section

Linguistic Structure

[Opening] [1]The oracle of Nineveh. The book of the vision of Nahum the Elkoshite.

A [2] A jealous and avenging God is the LORD; The LORD is avenging and wrathful. The LORD takes vengeance on His adversaries, And He reserves wrath for His enemies. [3] The LORD is slow to anger and great in power, And the LORD will by no means leave *the guilty* unpunished. In whirlwind and storm is His way, And clouds are the dust beneath His feet.

B [4] He rebukes the sea and makes it dry; He dries up all the rivers. Bashan and Carmel wither; The blossoms of Lebanon wither. [5] Mountains quake because of Him And the hills dissolve; Indeed the earth is upheaved by His presence, The world and all the inhabitants in it.

A' [6] Who can stand before His indignation? Who can endure the burning of His anger? His wrath is poured out like fire And the rocks are broken up by Him. [7] The LORD is good, A stronghold in the day of trouble, And He knows those who take refuge in Him. [8] But with an overflowing flood He will make a complete end of its site, And will pursue His enemies into darkness.

> A: Wrath of the LORD. B: Natural disasters.[4]

A [9] Whatever you devise against the LORD, He will make a complete end of it. Distress will not rise up twice.

> **B** [10] Like tangled thorns, And like those who are drunken with their drink, They are consumed As stubble completely withered.

A' [11] From you has gone forth One who plotted evil against the LORD, A wicked counselor.

> A: To devise evil. B: The LORD destroyed.[5]

---

[4] "Literary Structure (chiasm, Chiasmus) of Book of Nahum." Literary Structure (chiasm, Chiasmus) of Each Pericopes of Book of Nahum. Accessed September 22, 2017. http://www.bible.literarystructure.info/bible/34_Nahum_peric ope_e.html.

[5] IBID.

[The LORD says] [12] Thus says the LORD, "Though they are at full *strength* and likewise many, Even so, they will be cut off and pass away. Though I have afflicted you, I will afflict you no longer. So now, I will break his yoke bar from upon you, And I will tear off your shackles."

[The LORD says] [14] The LORD has issued a command concerning you: "Your name will no longer be perpetuated. I will cut off idol and image From the house of your gods. I will prepare your grave, For you are contemptible."

[15] Behold, on the mountains the feet of him who brings good news, Who announces peace! Celebrate your feasts, O Judah; Pay your vows. For never again will the wicked one pass through you; He is cut off completely.

Discussion

There are two chiasms in this chapter and two commands from the LORD. Verse 15 is included in chapter one in the English versions of the Bible. In the Hebrew version, it is the first verse of chapter two.

Questioning the Passage

1. Where was the city of Elkosh located? (v. 1)

   Elkosh was a city in the northern part of the Northern Kingdom of Israel.

2. What is the difference between being an adversary of the LORD and being an enemy of the LORD? (V. 2)

   The LORD takes vengeance against His adversaries. They are defined as the heathen nations who have or will destroy the land of Israel or have or will kill any of the LORD's chosen people (Rashi[6]). Vengeance is prohibited by the Torah. This applies only when the Jew takes vengeance against a

---

[6] Rabbi Solomon ben Isaac (Shlomo Yitzhaki), known as Rashi (based on an acronym of his Hebrew initials), is one of the most influential Jewish commentators in history. He was born in Troyes, Champagne, in northern France, in 1040. Source: http://www.myjewishlearning.com/article/who-was-rashi/

fellow Jew (Abarbanel[7]). Therefore, it is the LORD who will take vengeance for Israel, thus making a nation an enemy of Israel.

Being an adversary of the LORD means the LORD will take vengeance sooner rather than later. An enemy of the LORD is an adversary but one whom the LORD takes vengeance on in the future.[8]

3. What does it mean that the LORD is slow to anger? (v. 3)

---

[7] Don Isaac Abravanel was one of the greatest Jewish statesmen who played an important part in European history. At the same time he was not merely a loyal and strictly religious Jew, but a great scholar, Bible commentator and philosopher. He was the last of the long line of great Jewish leaders and heroes of the Spanish Golden Age. Source: http://www.chabad.org/library/article_cdo/aid/111855/jewish /Don-Isaac-Abravanel-The-Abarbanel.htm

[8] Scherman, Nosson, Meir Zlotowitz, Sheah Brander, and Menachem Davis. "Nahum Chapter One." In *The Prophets: The Later Prophets with a Commentary Anthologized from the Rabbinic Writings*. Brooklyn, NY: Mesorah Publications, 2013.

The Talmud, in the tractate Sanhedrin, says that the LORD is slow to bring punishment upon any people, thus giving them a chance to correct their ways and repent from their sins.

4. What does it mean that Bashan and Carmel will wither? (v. 4)

Bashan was a fertile pasture in the east, while Carmel was a fertile pasture in the west. When the LORD prevents rain from falling the vegetation on the grass lands dry up. This is a metaphor for what the LORD does to His adversaries. He destroys nation that oppose Him or try to hurt Israel.[9]

---

[9] IBID.

5. What does it mean that the blooms of Lebanon wither? (v. 4)

Literally, this means that the flowers that grow in Lebanon would wither like the pastures of Bashan and Carmel. According to Yoma 39b of the Talmud, Lebanon is a reference to Jerusalem (since Lebanon cedar trees were used in the construction of the Temple), and the flowers (or blooms) is a reference to a fruit that grew there. According to legend, King Solomon planted golden fruited trees in Jerusalem. The priests would collect the fruit when it fell off the trees, which gave them a food source.

6. What is the burning anger of the LORD? (v. 6)

Verse six is a set of repetitions where the author clarifies that once a nation is considered an adversary of the LORD that the LORD's answer will be poured out against the people of that nation.

7. What does the simile of "his wrath is poured out like fire" mean? (v. 6)

This is a reference to the ways the LORD has poured out His anger. Fire from the sky happened to Sodom and Gomorrah.

8. What does the symbolism of tangled thorns mean? (v. 10)

The Sages viewed this as a symbol of the strength of the Assyrians. Nahum prophesies that even though Assyrian is large and powerful, she cannot withstand the wrath of the LORD.

9. Who is Nahum taking about in verse 14?

The Targum of Nahum says in verse 14 that the words of the LORD are directed to the King of Assyria.

People's names

1. נָחוּם *Nachum* **Meaning:** an Israeli prophet

Name of places

1. נִינְוֵה *Nineveh* **Meaning:** capital of Assyria

2. בָּשָׁן *Bashan* **Meaning:** 'smooth,' a region east of the Jordan

3. כַּרְמֶל *Karmel* **Meaning:** a mountain promontory on the Mediterranean, also a city near Hebron

4. יְהוּדָה *Yehudah* **Meaning:** the southern kingdom

Scripture cross references

Verse 1 Isa 13:1; Isa 19:1; Jer 23:33, Jer 23:34; Hab 1:1; Zec 9:1; Mal 1:1; 2Ki 19:36; Jon 1:2; Nah 2:8; Zep 2:13

Verse 3 Exo 34:6, Exo 34:7; Neh 9:17; Psa 103:8; Exo 19:16; Isa 29:6

Verse 4 Exo 34:6, Exo 34:7; Neh 9:17; Psa 103:8; Exo 19:16; Isa 29:6; Psa 104:3; Isa 19:1

Verse 8 Isa 28:2, Isa 28:17f; Amo 8:8; Isa 13:9, Isa 13:10

Verse 12 Isa 10:16-19, Isa 10:33, 34; Lam 3:31, Lam 3:32

Verse 14 Job 18:17; Psa 109:13; Isa 14:22; Isa 46:1, Isa 46:2; Mic 5:13, Mic 5:14; Eze 32:22, Eze 32:23

Main/Center Point

The prophecy of Nahum was directed at the Assyrians. The first chapter tells us how furious the LORD was. He sent Jonah to warn the people of their sins. According to Jonah, the people complied and repented. That repentance was not permanent because Assyria continued to grow into one of the evilest nations in the Middle East. The LORD was angry, perhaps because he saw how quickly the Ninevites turned back to their evil ways. It was time for the LORD to step in and show them His anger, and his judgment against them. The anger was fueled by what the Assyrians did to the Northern Kingdom of Israel. Some scholars believe that the Assyrian invasion was a punishment from the LORD about the sins of the people of the Northern Kingdom. Perhaps it was not. Perhaps the Assyrian invasion and destruction of the Northern Kingdom was simply Assyria capturing more territories and peoples and that is why the LORD was so angry with them.

Thoughts

Looking at the prophecy of Jonah, how could the LORD not do something about the fact that Assyria repented before the LORD and then turned back to their evil ways? That is the story of Israel too. Therefore, could this prophecy from Nahum be directed to Israel? The Northern and Southern kingdoms had prophets from the LORD dwelling in their land and they would revert to following the LORD. Sometimes Israel did not follow the LORD.

Now the great empire of Assyria was going to be destroyed by the LORD because they listened for a while to a prophet of the LORD, then returned to their evil ways If the LORD would destroy Assyria for not obeying, would not the LORD punish Israel? The people of Judah should have taken heed when Assyria was destroyed.

Perhaps we should heed Nahum's prophecy as a warning to us today.

Nahum Chapter 2

Language

New American Standard 1995	Hebrew
1 The one who scatters has come up against you. Man the fortress, watch the road; Strengthen your back, summon all your strength. 2 For the LORD will restore the splendor of Jacob Like the splendor of Israel, Even though devastators have devastated them And destroyed their vine branches. 3 The shields of his mighty men are colored red, The warriors are dressed in scarlet, The chariots are	¹הִנֵּה עַל־הֶהָרִים רַגְלֵי מְבַשֵּׂר מַשְׁמִיעַ שָׁלוֹם חָגִּי יְהוּדָה חַגַּיִךְ שַׁלְּמִי נְדָרָיִךְ כִּי לֹא יוֹסִיף עוֹד (לַעֲבוֹר־)[לַעֲבָר־]בָּךְ בְּלִיַּעַל כֻּלֹּה נִכְרָת: ²עָלָה מֵפִיץ עַל־פָּנַיִךְ נָצוֹר מְצֻרָה צַפֵּה־דֶרֶךְ חַזֵּק מָתְנַיִם אַמֵּץ כֹּחַ מְאֹד: ³כִּי שָׁב יְהוָה אֶת־גְּאוֹן יַעֲקֹב כִּגְאוֹן יִשְׂרָאֵל כִּי בְקָקוּם בֹּקְקִים וּזְמֹרֵיהֶם שִׁחֵתוּ: ⁴מָגֵן גִּבֹּרֵיהוּ מְאָדָּם אַנְשֵׁי־חַיִל מְתֻלָּעִים בְּאֵשׁ־פְּלָדוֹת הָרֶכֶב בְּיוֹם הֲכִינוֹ וְהַבְּרֹשִׁים הָרְעָלוּ: ⁵בַּחוּצוֹת יִתְהוֹלְלוּ הָרֶכֶב יִשְׁתַּקְשְׁקוּן

enveloped in flashing steel When he is prepared to march, And the cypress spears are brandished.

4 The chariots race madly in the streets, They rush wildly in the squares, Their appearance is like torches, They dash to and fro like lightning flashes.

5 He remembers his nobles; They stumble in their march, They hurry to her wall, And the mantelet is set up.

6 The gates of the rivers are opened And the palace is dissolved.

7 It is fixed: She is stripped, she is carried away, And her handmaids are moaning like the

בִּרְחֹבוֹת מַרְאֵיהֶן כַּלַּפִּידִם כַּבְּרָקִים יְרוֹצֵצוּ:
6 יִזְכֹּר אַדִּירָיו יִכָּשְׁלוּ (בַהֲלֹכוּתָם) [בַּהֲלִיכָתָם] יְמַהֲרוּ חוֹמָתָהּ וְהֻכַן הַסֹּכֵךְ:
7 שַׁעֲרֵי הַנְּהָרוֹת נִפְתָּחוּ וְהַהֵיכָל נָמוֹג:
8 וְהֻצַּב גֻּלְּתָה הֹעֲלָתָה וְאַמְהֹתֶיהָ מְנַהֲגוֹת כְּקוֹל יוֹנִים מְתֹפְפֹת עַל־לִבְבֵהֶן:
9 וְנִינְוֵה כִבְרֵכַת־מַיִם מִימֵי הִיא וְהֵמָּה נָסִים עִמְדוּ עֲמֹדוּ וְאֵין מַפְנֶה:
10 בֹּזּוּ כֶסֶף בֹּזּוּ זָהָב וְאֵין קֵצֶה לַתְּכוּנָה כָּבֹד מִכֹּל כְּלִי חֶמְדָּה:
11 בּוּקָה וּמְבוּקָה וּמְבֻלָּקָה וְלֵב נָמֵס וּפִק בִּרְכַּיִם וְחַלְחָלָה בְּכָל־מָתְנַיִם וּפְנֵי כֻלָּם קִבְּצוּ פָארוּר:
12 אַיֵּה מְעוֹן אֲרָיוֹת וּמִרְעֶה הוּא לַכְּפִרִים אֲשֶׁר הָלַךְ אַרְיֵה לָבִיא

sound of doves, Beating on their breasts.

8 Though Nineveh was like a pool of water throughout her days, Now they are fleeing; "Stop, stop," But no one turns back.

9 Plunder the silver! Plunder the gold! For there is no limit to the treasure-- Wealth from every kind of desirable object.

10 She is emptied! Yes, she is desolate and waste! Hearts are melting and knees knocking! Also anguish is in the whole body And all their faces are grown pale!

11 Where is the den of the lions And the feeding place of the young lions, Where

שָׁם גּוּר אַרְיֵה וְאֵין מַחֲרִיד:
13 אַרְיֵה טֹרֵף בְּדֵי גְרוֹתָיו וּמְחַנֵּק לְלִבְאֹתָיו וַיְמַלֵּא־טֶרֶף חֹרָיו וּמְעֹנֹתָיו טְרֵפָה:
14 הִנְנִי אֵלַיִךְ נְאֻם יְהוָה צְבָאוֹת וְהִבְעַרְתִּי בֶעָשָׁן רִכְבָּהּ וּכְפִירַיִךְ תֹּאכַל חָרֶב וְהִכְרַתִּי מֵאֶרֶץ טַרְפֵּךְ וְלֹא־יִשָּׁמַע עוֹד קוֹל מַלְאָכֵכֵה: ס

the lion, lioness and lion's cub prowled, With nothing to disturb them? [12] The lion tore enough for his cubs, Killed enough for his lionesses, And filled his lairs with prey And his dens with torn flesh. [13] "Behold, I am against you," declares the LORD of hosts. "I will burn up her chariots in smoke, a sword will devour your young lions; I will cut off your prey from the land, and no longer will the voice of your messengers be heard."	

Process of Discovery

Linguistics Section

Linguistic Structure

A [15] Behold, on the mountains the feet of him who brings good news, Who announces peace! Celebrate your feasts, O Judah; Pay your vows. For never again will the wicked one pass through you; He is cut off completely.[1]The one who scatters has come up against you. Man the fortress, watch the road; Strengthen your back, summon all *your* strength.

B [2] For the LORD will restore the splendor of Jacob Like the splendor of Israel, Even though devastators have devastated them And destroyed their vine branches.

A' [3] The shields of his mighty men are *colored* red, The warriors are dressed in scarlet, The chariots are *enveloped* in flashing steel When he is prepared *to march*, And the cypress *spears* are brandished.

A: Good news. B: Attack of enemies.[10]

A [4] The chariots race madly in the streets, They rush wildly in the squares, Their appearance is like torches, They dash to and fro like lightning

---

[10] "Literary Structure (chiasm, Chiasmus) of Book of Nahum." Literary Structure (chiasm, Chiasmus) of Each Pericopes of Book of Nahum. Accessed September 22, 2017. http://www.bible.literarystructure.info/bible/34_Nahum_peric ope_e.html.

flashes. [5] He remembers his nobles; They stumble in their march, They hurry to her wall, And the mantelet is set up. [6] The gates of the rivers are opened And the palace is dissolved.

B [7] It is fixed: She is stripped, she is carried away, And her handmaids are moaning like the sound of doves, Beating on their breasts. [8] Though Nineveh *was* like a pool of water throughout her days, Now they are fleeing; "Stop, stop," But no one turns back.

B' [9] Plunder the silver! Plunder the gold! For there is no limit to the treasure-- Wealth from every kind of desirable object. [10] She is emptied! Yes, she is desolate and waste! Hearts are melting and knees knocking! Also anguish is in the whole body And all their faces are grown pale

A' [11] Where is the den of the lions And the feeding place of the young lions, Where the lion, lioness and lion's cub prowled, With nothing to disturb *them*? [12] The lion tore enough for his cubs, Killed *enough* for his lionesses, And filled his lairs with prey And his dens with torn flesh. [13] "Behold, I am against you," declares the LORD of hosts. "I will burn up her chariots in smoke, a sword will devour your young lions; I will cut off your prey from the land, and no longer will the voice of your messengers be heard."

A: Destruction. B: Robbery.[11]

Discussion

There are two chiasms in this chapter. The hope that the prophet offers is in this chapter. Verse 15 from chapter one is included in chapter two because it is chapter two verse one in the Tanakh and it is a part of the first chiasm of chapter two.

---

[11] "Literary Structure (chiasm, Chiasmus) of Book of Nahum." Literary Structure (chiasm, Chiasmus) of Each Pericopes of Book of Nahum. Accessed September 22, 2017. http://www.bible.literarystructure.info/bible/34_Nahum_peric ope_e.html.

Questioning the Passage

1. Who is announcing peace in chapter one verse 15?

   It is not clear who announced the peace. The peace being announced is that Sennacherib, the emperor of Assyria was dead and that Assyria had been defeated by the Babylonians. The people that were expelled from their lands could return home. When Assyria conquered a land the people of the land were spread out into the Empire. The Babylonians did not do that. They would keep people together in Exile, if they were rebellious.[12]

---

[12] Scherman, Nosson, Meir Zlotowitz, Sheah Brander, and Menachem Davis. "Nahum Chapter Two." In *The Prophets: The Later Prophets with a Commentary Anthologized from the Rabbinic Writings*. Brooklyn, NY: Mesorah Publications, 2013.

2. Why were they told to celebrate their feasts? (chapter 1, v. 15)

    When the Assyrians took the northern kingdom, the people in the north could not celebrate the feasts of the LORD. The Hebrew people from the north could not go to the Temple in Jerusalem to worship. Now they could, unfortunately the people were scattered through Assyria and never returned to the area of the Northern Kingdom nor to Jerusalem.

3. Who is the wicked one? (chapter 1, v. 15)

    Sennacherib and his children are the wicked ones spoken of in this passage.[13]

____

[13] IBID.

4. Who is the one who scatters? (v. 1)

   The one who scatters is Sennacherib.

5. What is the difference between the splendor of Jacob and the splendor of Israel? (v. 2)

   The splendor of Jacob is found in the success of the Southern Kingdom. After Assyria fell, Judea (the splendor of Israel) wiggled away from the control of the Empire. It would take time for the Babylonians to move to the south and regain the territories of the former Assyrian empire.

6. What is the symbolism of the vine branches? (v. 2)

   When the Assyrians invaded the Northern Kingdom, they destroyed the cities of the land. They burned everything they could. The vine branches are the symbol of beauty that was the land before the invasion.

7. What is the symbolism of red? (v. 3)
   The mighty men were the soldiers of the Babylonian army and red was the blood that stained their swords and shields.[14]

8. What is the symbolism of the color scarlet? (v. 3)
   The color scarlet was the color used by the high-ranking officers in the Babylonian army to identify themselves.

9. What does it mean that the chariots are enveloped in flashing steel? (v. 3)

---

[14] IBID.

When the chariot's wheels of steel move quickly across the stone roads sparks fly would off the wheels. These sparks look like flashing steel.[15]

10. What does "her wall" mean in verse five?

This reference is to the walls of Nineveh.

11. What are the gates of the rivers? (v. 6)

The gates of Nineveh were near the rivers that surrounded the city.

12. What is the meaning of verse nine and ten?

---

[15] IBID.

The Babylonian army took all the valuables from the city of Nineveh and then destroyed the city.

13. What does the metaphor "den of lions" mean in verse 13?

The LORD is stronger than any country on the Earth, even the lion. The lion was considered the strongest animal that lived in the Middle East.

Scripture cross references

Verse 1	Jer 51:20-23
Verse 3	Eze 23:14, Eze 23:15; Job 39:23
Verse 8	Jer 46:5; Jer 47:3

Main/Center Point

Nahum prophecies the destruction of the city of Nineveh by the Babylonian army. He also insures that the people understand that the LORD sent the Babylonian army to destroy Nineveh because the city turned to the LORD through the prophet Jonah, then turned back to their evil ways, thus insulting and angering the LORD.

Culture Section

Discussion

According to the Targum, the female that is being referred in verse 7 is a reference to the Queen of Nineveh.

There is a legend that most of the royal household of the Assyrian empire fled to the north, to what today is called Kurdistan, and their descendant live there even today.[16]

---

[16] Errico, Rocco A., and George M. Lamsa. "Nahum Chapter Two." In *Aramaic Light on Ezekiel, Daniel, and the Minor Prophets: A Commentary Based on the Aramaic Language and Ancient Near Eastern Customs*. Smyrna, GA: Noohra Foundation, 2012.

Thoughts

A question would be, did the LORD send the Babylonians because of Jonah, or because they destroyed the ten northern tribes of Israel? By listening to Jonah with repentance and then doing as they pleased, the Assyrians agitated the LORD. Therefore, the LORD sent the Babylonians to defeat the Assyrians. If the Assyrian invasion of the north is viewed as the LORD's punishment of the north, then the anger of the LORD toward Assyria was because of their repentance of their sins and then being evil again. Either way, the LORD sent the Babylonians to destroy the Assyrian empire and the city of Nineveh.

This book also tells us that the idea of monotheism is a strong part of the Hebrew people's theology at the time of its writing. The LORD now judges other people than just Israel and Judah. The people of Nineveh were offered a chance at redemption through Jonah. They accepted it but then returned to their evil ways. So, the LORD punished the Assyrians, destroying the city and killing the King and queen.

Nahum Chapter 3

Language

New American Standard 1995	Hebrew
¹ Woe to the bloody city, completely full of lies *and* pillage; *Her* prey never departs. ² The noise of the whip, The noise of the rattling of the wheel, Galloping horses And bounding chariots! ³ Horsemen charging, Swords flashing, spears gleaming, Many slain, a mass of corpses, And countless dead bodies-- They stumble over the dead bodies! ⁴ *All* because of the many harlotries of	הֹוי עִיר דָּמִים כֻּלָּהּ כַּחַשׁ פֶּרֶק מְלֵאָה לֹא יָמִישׁ טָרֶף: ²קֹול שֹׁוט וְקֹול רַעַשׁ אֹופָן וְסוּס דֹּהֵר וּמֶרְכָּבָה מְרַקֵּדָה: ³ פָּרָשׁ מַעֲלֶה וְלַהַב חֶרֶב וּבְרַק חֲנִית וְרֹב חָלָל וְכֹבֶד פָּגֶר וְאֵין קֵצֶה לַגְּוִיָּה (יְכָשְׁלוּ) [וְכָשְׁלוּ] בִּגְוִיָּתָם: ⁴ מֵרֹב זְנוּנֵי זֹונָה טֹובַת חֵן בַּעֲלַת כְּשָׁפִים הַמֹּכֶרֶת גֹּויִם בִּזְנוּנֶיהָ וּמִשְׁפָּחֹות בִּכְשָׁפֶיהָ: ⁵ הִנְנִי אֵלַיִךְ נְאֻם יְהוָה צְבָאֹות וְגִלֵּיתִי שׁוּלַיִךְ עַל־פָּנָיִךְ וְהַרְאֵיתִי גֹויִם מַעְרֵךְ וּמַמְלָכֹות קְלֹונֵךְ:

the harlot, The charming one, the mistress of sorceries, Who sells nations by her harlotries And families by her sorceries.

5 "Behold, I am against you," declares the LORD of hosts; "And I will lift up your skirts over your face, And show to the nations your nakedness And to the kingdoms your disgrace.

6 "I will throw filth on you And make you vile, And set you up as a spectacle.

7 "And it will come about that all who see you Will shrink from you and say, 'Nineveh is devastated! Who will grieve for her?'

וְהִשְׁלַכְתִּי עָלַיִךְ 6 שִׁקֻּצִים וְנִבַּלְתִּיךְ וְשַׂמְתִּיךְ כְּרֹאִי:

וְהָיָה כָל־רֹאַיִךְ יִדּוֹד 7 מִמֵּךְ וְאָמַר שָׁדְּדָה נִינְוֵה מִי יָנוּד לָהּ מֵאַיִן אֲבַקֵּשׁ מְנַחֲמִים לָךְ:

הֲתֵיטְבִי מִנֹּא אָמוֹן 8 הַיֹּשְׁבָה בַּיְאֹרִים מַיִם סָבִיב לָהּ אֲשֶׁר־חֵיל יָם מִיָּם חוֹמָתָהּ:

כּוּשׁ עָצְמָה וּמִצְרַיִם 9 וְאֵין קֵצֶה פּוּט וְלוּבִים הָיוּ בְּעֶזְרָתֵךְ:

גַּם־הִיא לַגֹּלָה 10 הָלְכָה בַשֶּׁבִי גַּם עֹלָלֶיהָ יְרֻטְּשׁוּ בְּרֹאשׁ כָּל־חוּצוֹת וְעַל־נִכְבַּדֶּיהָ יַדּוּ גוֹרָל וְכָל־גְּדוֹלֶיהָ רֻתְּקוּ בַזִּקִּים:

גַּם־אַתְּ תִּשְׁכְּרִי תְּהִי 11 נַעֲלָמָה גַּם־אַתְּ תְּבַקְשִׁי מָעוֹז מֵאוֹיֵב:

כָּל־מִבְצָרַיִךְ תְּאֵנִים 12 עִם־בִּכּוּרִים אִם־יִנּוֹעוּ וְנָפְלוּ עַל־פִּי אוֹכֵל:

הִנֵּה עַמֵּךְ נָשִׁים 13 בְּקִרְבֵּךְ לְאֹיְבַיִךְ פָּתוֹחַ

Where will I seek comforters for you?"

⁸ Are you better than No-amon, Which was situated by the waters of the Nile, With water surrounding her, Whose rampart *was* the sea, Whose wall *consisted* of the sea?

⁹ Ethiopia was *her* might, And Egypt too, without limits. Put and Lubim were among her helpers.

¹⁰ Yet she became an exile, She went into captivity; Also her small children were dashed to pieces At the head of every street; They cast lots for her honorable men, And all her great men were bound with fetters.

¹¹ You too will become drunk, You

נִפְתְּחוּ שַׁעֲרֵי אַרְצֵךְ אָכְלָה אֵשׁ בְּרִיחָיִךְ:
¹⁴ מֵי מָצוֹר שַׁאֲבִי־לָךְ חַזְּקִי מִבְצָרָיִךְ בֹּאִי בַטִּיט וְרִמְסִי בַחֹמֶר הַחֲזִיקִי מַלְבֵּן:
¹⁵ שָׁם תֹּאכְלֵךְ אֵשׁ תַּכְרִיתֵךְ חֶרֶב תֹּאכְלֵךְ כַּיָּלֶק הִתְכַּבֵּד כַּיֶּלֶק הִתְכַּבְּדִי כָּאַרְבֶּה:
¹⁶ הִרְבֵּית רֹכְלַיִךְ מִכּוֹכְבֵי הַשָּׁמָיִם יֶלֶק פָּשַׁט וַיָּעֹף:
¹⁷ מִנְּזָרַיִךְ כָּאַרְבֶּה וְטַפְסְרַיִךְ כְּגוֹב גֹּבָי הַחוֹנִים בַּגְּדֵרוֹת בְּיוֹם קָרָה שֶׁמֶשׁ זָרְחָה וְנוֹדַד וְלֹא־נוֹדַע מְקוֹמוֹ אַיָּם:
¹⁸ נָמוּ רֹעֶיךָ מֶלֶךְ אַשּׁוּר יִשְׁכְּנוּ אַדִּירֶיךָ נָפֹשׁוּ עַמְּךָ עַל־הֶהָרִים וְאֵין מְקַבֵּץ:
¹⁹ אֵין־כֵּהָה לְשִׁבְרֶךָ נַחְלָה מַכָּתֶךָ כֹּל שֹׁמְעֵי שִׁמְעֲךָ תָּקְעוּ כַף עָלֶיךָ כִּי עַל־מִי

will be hidden. You too will search for a refuge from the enemy. 12 All your fortifications are fig trees with ripe fruit-- When shaken, they fall into the eater's mouth. 13 Behold, your people are women in your midst! The gates of your land are opened wide to your enemies; Fire consumes your gate bars. 14 Draw for yourself water for the siege! Strengthen your fortifications! Go into the clay and tread the mortar! Take hold of the brick mold! 15 There fire will consume you, The sword will cut you	לֹא־עָבְרָה רָעָתְךָ תָּמִיד׃

down; It will consume you as the locust *does*. Multiply yourself like the creeping locust, Multiply yourself like the swarming locust.
16 You have increased your traders more than the stars of heaven-- The creeping locust strips and flies away.
17 Your guardsmen are like the swarming locust. Your marshals are like hordes of grasshoppers Settling in the stone walls on a cold day. The sun rises and they flee, And the place where they are is not known.
18 Your shepherds are sleeping, O king of Assyria; Your nobles are lying

down. Your people are scattered on the mountains And there is no one to regather *them*. [19] There is no relief for your breakdown, Your wound is incurable. All who hear about you Will clap *their* hands over you, For on whom has not your evil passed continually?	

Process of Discovery

Linguistics Section

Linguistic Structure

A [1] Woe to the bloody city, completely full of lies *and* pillage; *Her* prey never departs. [2] The noise of the whip, The noise of the rattling of the wheel, Galloping horses And bounding chariots! [3] Horsemen charging, Swords flashing, spears gleaming, **Many slain**, a mass of corpses, And countless dead bodies-- They stumble over the dead bodies! [4] *All* because of the many harlotries of the harlot, The charming one, the mistress of sorceries, Who sells nations by her harlotries And families by her sorceries.

B [5] "Behold, I am against you," declares the LORD of hosts; "And I will lift up your skirts over your face, And show to the nations your nakedness And to the kingdoms your disgrace. [6] "I will throw filth on you And make you vile, And set you up as a spectacle. [7] "And it will come about that all who see you Will shrink from you and say, 'Nineveh is devastated! Who will grieve for her?' Where will I seek comforters for you?" [8] Are you better than No-amon, Which was situated by the waters of the Nile, With water surrounding her, Whose rampart *was* the sea, Whose wall *consisted* of the sea? [9] Ethiopia was *her* might, And Egypt too, without limits. Put and Lubim were among her helpers. [10] Yet she became an exile, She went into captivity; Also her small children were dashed to pieces At the head of every street; They cast lots for her honorable men, And all her great men were bound with fetters.

B' [11] You too will become drunk, You will be hidden. You too will search for a refuge from the enemy. [12] All your fortifications are fig trees with ripe fruit-- When shaken, they fall into the eater's mouth. [13] Behold, your people are women in your midst! The gates of your land are opened wide to your enemies; Fire consumes your gate bars. [14] Draw for yourself water for the siege! Strengthen your fortifications! Go into the clay and tread the mortar! Take hold of the brick mold! [15] There fire will consume you, The sword will cut you down; It will consume you as the locust *does*. Multiply yourself like the creeping locust, Multiply yourself like the swarming locust. [16] You have increased your traders more than the stars of heaven-- The creeping locust strips and flies away. [17] Your guardsmen are like the swarming locust. Your marshals are like hordes of grasshoppers Settling in the stone walls on a cold day. The sun rises and they flee, And the place where they are is not known.

A' [18] Your shepherds are sleeping, O king of Assyria; Your nobles are lying down. Your people are scattered on the mountains And there is no one to regather *them*. [19] There is no relief for your breakdown, **Your wound is incurable.** All who hear about you Will clap *their* hands over you, For on whom has not your evil passed continually?

Discussion

The simple chiasm is a declaration from the LORD that the city if Nineveh will be brutally destroyed.

Questioning the Passage

1. Why call Nineveh the city of blood? (v. 1)

   Nahum continues his prophecy of the destruction of Nineveh. The city is called the "city of blood" because of all death that occurred when the Babylonians invaded the city. The reference could also refer to the fact that Assyria murdered a large multitude of people during the reign of the Empire.

2. What is the prey of the city? (v. 1)

    The prey of the city was all the wealth and people the Assyrians took from the nations they conquered.[17]

3. Who is the mistress of sorceries? (v. 4)

    In the Targum, the references in verse four tell us that when the Babylonians attacked the city, there would be chaos and eventually anarchy in the city. Harlots practiced sorcery and when a city was attacked, the harlots would help the attackers.

4. What is the symbolism of "I will lift up you skirts over your face and show to

---

[17] Scherman, Nosson, Meir Zlotowitz, Sheah Brander, and Menachem Davis. "Nahum Chapter Two." In *The Prophets: The Later Prophets with a Commentary Anthologized from the Rabbinic Writings*. Brooklyn, NY: Mesorah Publications, 2013.

the nations your nakedness" mean? (v. 5)

The symbolism of this phrase is that the LORD will reveal the shame of the sins of the Assyrians to the world and there would be justice for those who had to endure their sin.

5. What is the symbolism of verse six?

   The symbolism is that the LORD will make the nations of the known world view the Assyrians as enemies who deserve death for the sinful and evil things that they did.

6. Why, in verse nine, is there a reference to Egypt and Ethiopia?

   The nations in verse nine were allies of the Assyrians. When the LORD's justice came to Assyria, her allies did not come to her aid. It is possible that the large distance between Egypt and Assyria would have made it difficult for Egypt to come to the aid of the Assyrians. Also, if a large Egyptian army moved north to Nineveh, it would have left Egypt vulnerable to invasion.

7. What is the symbolism of the fig tree in verse 12?

   The symbolism here says that the impregnable fortresses of the Assyrians will be easily conquered and plundered by Nebuchadnezzar, the emperor of the Babylonian empire[18] .

8. Why is symbolism of locust and grasshoppers in verse 17?

Locust will cling to the city walls during the night, but they scatter when the sun rises. The guardsmen of Nineveh will scatter when the Babylonian army arrives at Nineveh because of their fear.

Main/Center Point

Chapter two is about preparing the Babylonian army. Chapter three describes the attack on the city of Nineveh and the Empire.

---

[18] IBID.

Name of places

1. נא *No* **Meaning:** an Egyptian city

2. מִצְרַיִם *Mitsrayim* **Meaning:** a son of Ham, also his descendants. and their country in N.W. Africa

3. פוּט *Put* **Meaning:** a son of Ham, also his descendants and their land

4. לוּבִים *Lubim* **Meaning:** inhabitants of North Africa

Scripture cross references

Verse 2   Job 39:22-25; Jer 47:3

Verse 6   Job 9:31; Job 30:8; Mal 2:9; Isa 14:16; Jer 51:37

Verse 10   Isa 19:4; Isa 20:4; Psa 137:9; Isa 13:16; Hos 13:16; Lam 2:19; Joe 3:3; Oba 1:11

Verse 11   Isa 49:26; Jer 25:27; Isa 2:10, Isa 2:19; Hos 10:8; Isa 49:26; Jer 25:27; Isa 2:10, Isa 2:19; Hos 10:8

Verse 14   2Ch 32:3, 2Ch 32:4

Verse 17   Rev 9:7; Jer 51:27

Verse 18   Psa 76:5, Psa 76:6; Isa 56:10; Jer 51:57; Jer 50:18; 1Ki 22:17; Isa 13:14

Culture Section

Questioning the passage

1. "Your people in the midst of you are women" (v. 13) means?

   This is a Near Eastern expression meaning that the people are cowards. When the Babylonians invaded, Nahum said that the Assyrians will become cowards and they will run.[19]

---

[19] Errico, Rocco A., and George M. Lamsa. "Nahum Chapter Three." In *Aramaic Light on Ezekiel, Daniel, and the Minor Prophets:*

Thoughts

The final words of Nahum are a prophecy about what was going to be the assault on the Assyrian Empire and Nineveh by the Babylonians. The Babylonian army was so large that the warriors of Assyria became cowardly and ran. The city of Nineveh was going to be overrun and taken. The Assyrian empire did fall to the Babylonians.

Today we should learn from this book that the LORD gets angry with people who repent of their sines then return to their sinful ways.

A Commentary Based on the Aramaic Language and Ancient Near Eastern Customs. Smyrna, GA: Noohra Foundation, 2012.

Bibliography

Errico, R. A. (2000). *Aramaic Light on the Gospel of Matthew*. Santa Fe, NM: Noohra Foundation.

Mindel, N. (2017, September 18). *Don Isaac Abravanel - "The Abarbanel"*. Retrieved from Chabad.org: http://www.chabad.org/library/article_cdo/aid/111855/jewish/Don-Isaac-Abravanel-The-Abarbanel.htm

Rashi. (2017, September 18). Retrieved from My Jewish Learning: http://www.myjewishlearning.com/article/who-was-rashi/

Scherman, N. M. (2013). *The Prophets: The later prophets with a commentary anthologized from the Rabbinic writings*. Brookyln: NY: Mesorah Publications.